Salmon

by Sylvia M. James
Illustrated by Paul Bachem

For my children Ronald Isaiah and Rachel Alease—S.M.J.

Acknowledgments:

Photo research by Sylvia M. James

PHOTO CREDITS:© The Stock Market/Kennan Ward, 1994: front cover, p. 10; © Gary Vestal/Tony Stone Images: p. 3; © The Stock Market/Zefa Germany, 1994: p. 5; ANIMALS ANIMALS © Victoria McCormick: pp. 9, 11, 19; ANIMALS ANIMALS © Ted Levin: p. 12; ANIMALS ANIMALS © Jose Schell: p. 14; © Natalie Fobes/Tony Stone Images: p. 16; ANIMALS ANIMALS © Lynn Stone: p. 20; EARTH SCENES © Ken Cole: p. 22; EARTH SCENES © Philip Hart: p. 24; EARTH SCENES © Francis Lepine: p. 25; ANIMALS ANIMALS © John Stern: p. 27; ANIMALS ANIMALS ©Breck P. Kent: p. 28; ©David Woodfall/Tony Stone Images: p. 29.

For information contact:

MONDO Publishing

980 Avenue of the Americas

New York, New York 10018

Visit our website at http://www.mondopub.com

Printed in China

07 08   9 8 7 6 5 4

ISBN 1-57255-805-9 (pb) ISBN 1-57255-806-7 (BB)

Design by ARLENE SCHLEIFER GOLDBERG

Library of Congress Cataloging-in-Publication Data

James, Sylvia M.
    Salmon / by Sylvia M. James ; illustrated by Paul Bachem.
        p. cm.
    ISBN 1-57255-805-9 (pbk.) -- ISBN 1-57255-806-7
    1. Salmon--Juvenile literature. [1. Salmon.] I. Bachem, Paul, ill. II. Title.

QL638.S2 J338 2000
579.5st6--dc21

00-042707

How Many Kinds of Salmon Are in the Ocean?

Name	Weight	Length	Habitat
Atlantic	84 pounds (38 kg)	5 feet (1.5 m)	Atlantic Ocean
Cherry	9 pounds (4.1 kg)	23 inches (58 cm)	Pacific Ocean
Chinook/ King	100 pounds (45 kg)	56 inches (1.4 m)	Pacific Ocean
Chum	9 pounds (4.1 kg)	25 inches (63 cm)	Pacific Ocean
Coho	10 pounds (4.5 kg)	24 inches (61 cm)	Pacific Ocean
Pink	4 pounds (1.8 kg)	20 inches (51 cm)	Pacific Ocean
Sockeye	6 pounds (2.7 kg)	25 inches (63 cm)	Pacific Ocean
Steelhead	9 pounds (4.1 kg)	24 inches (61 cm)	Pacific Ocean

Atlantic

Cherry

Chinook

Chum

Coho

Pink

Sockeye

Steelhead

Index

Contents

What Are Salmon?

Each spring and fall, millions of wriggling silver fish begin an amazing journey. They leave the salty ocean and swim into cold, bubbling rivers. Some hurl their bodies into the air to cross waterfalls. They leap, twist, and flip in the water as they swim upstream. These incredible fish are salmon. The name "salmon" means "leaper."

Atlantic salmon leap over a waterfall.

How Many Kinds of Salmon Are There?

Although there are seven kinds of salmon in the Pacific Ocean, there is only one kind that swims in the Atlantic Ocean. The Atlantic salmon lives in the North Atlantic—from Greenland to Cape Cod. It is also found in Europe—from Russia to Great Britain, France, Spain, and Portugal. The Atlantic salmon may live 10 years and grow to 5 feet (1.5 m) in length and weigh 84 pounds (38 kg). Most are much smaller, usually between 3–20 pounds (1.4–9.9 kg).

Atlantic Salmon

Sockeye Salmon

Coho Salmon

Chum Salmon

Chinook Salmon

Steelhead Salmon

Pink Salmon

Cherry Salmon

All Pacific salmon are found in the waters around the United States, Canada, and Asia, except for the cherry, which lives near Japan and Korea. The largest Pacific salmon is the chinook or king salmon. It may reach over 100 pounds (45 kg). However, most chinooks are about 22 pounds (10 kg) and 32 inches (91 cm). The smallest Pacific species is the pink, which weighs only 4 pounds (1.8 kg) and is 20 inches (51 cm) long.

What Makes Salmon Special?

Salmon are unusual fish. They hatch in freshwater rivers and streams. But they live most of their lives in the ocean. All salmon return to fresh water to lay their eggs. To do this, they swim upstream. When salmon leave the ocean to begin "running upward," they always return to the stream where they were hatched. This birthplace is called the home stream.

Pink salmon push and shove to reach their home stream.

Sockeye salmon become bright red as they migrate upstream.

How Do Salmon Find Their Home Stream?

Scientists think the home stream has a special smell that the salmon recognize. This odor may come from the dirt, plants, and even the animals in the water. Some scientists think the sun helps the salmon, too. They do not understand exactly how all of these clues help salmon with their migration.

This pink salmon has found its home stream.

What Is the Salmon Run?

A salmon run is a long journey that is sometimes called a migration. The Atlantic salmon begins its run in autumn. It spends the first three years of its life in the Atlantic Ocean, feeding and growing into an adult. Next, the Atlantic salmon travels over 100 miles (107 km) to its home stream to spawn, or lay its eggs. Once it enters the river, it does not eat. Spawning takes place from October to December.

Atlantic Salmon Spawning

1. When adult salmon arrive in rivers to spawn, they lose their silvery color. The male's jaw becomes long and curved. Now, the male cannot eat or close its mouth.

2. The female salmon digs a large nest, called a redd, using her strong tail. The redd is 10 feet long (3.05 m) by 3–4 feet wide (0.9–1.2 m).

3. Males spread their fins and shake their bodies to attract females. They shove each other with their snouts, trying to chase other males away.

4. The female chooses the strongest male. The pair swims side by side as she prepares to lay her eggs.

5. A female may lay 800 eggs for every pound she weighs. This means that a 10-pound Atlantic salmon may lay 8,000 eggs! Some females lay up to 30,000 eggs.

6. The male fertilizes the eggs as they are laid. The female uses her tail to cover the eggs with pebbles.

These Atlantic salmon will make a nest beneath the gravel.

The female Atlantic salmon may make other nests but a different male will fertilize the eggs in each nest. After mating with just one female, the male is usually so tired that he dies. A small number returns to the sea with the females. These males come back again to spawn in their home stream the next year. Females may return two or three years in a row to spawn before dying.

How Do Baby Salmon Grow?

In the redd, thousands of sticky eggs remain hidden under the gravel during the winter months. The eggs are the size of small peas when laid. In the spring, the baby salmon hatch out of the eggs.

These coho salmon eggs are magnified and appear about four times larger than their actual size.

The fertilized egg begins to
develop under the gravel.

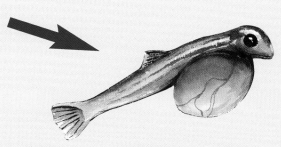

Baby salmon are called alevins. They have a yolk sac
attached to their bellies to provide food.

When the young salmon grow scales and become
silver, they are called smolts. Smolts leave streams
and rivers and begin their journey to the ocean. The
smolts remain in the ocean for at least a year,
feeding on shrimp and young crabs.

Babies larger than 1 inch (2.50 cm) are called fry.
Fry squirm out of the gravel and slowly grow by
eating baby insects.

At 4 inches long (10 cm), the salmon are called parr.
They have dark stripes on their brownish bodies
known as parr marks and feed on insects and small
fish. The parr remain in fresh water for 2–3 years.

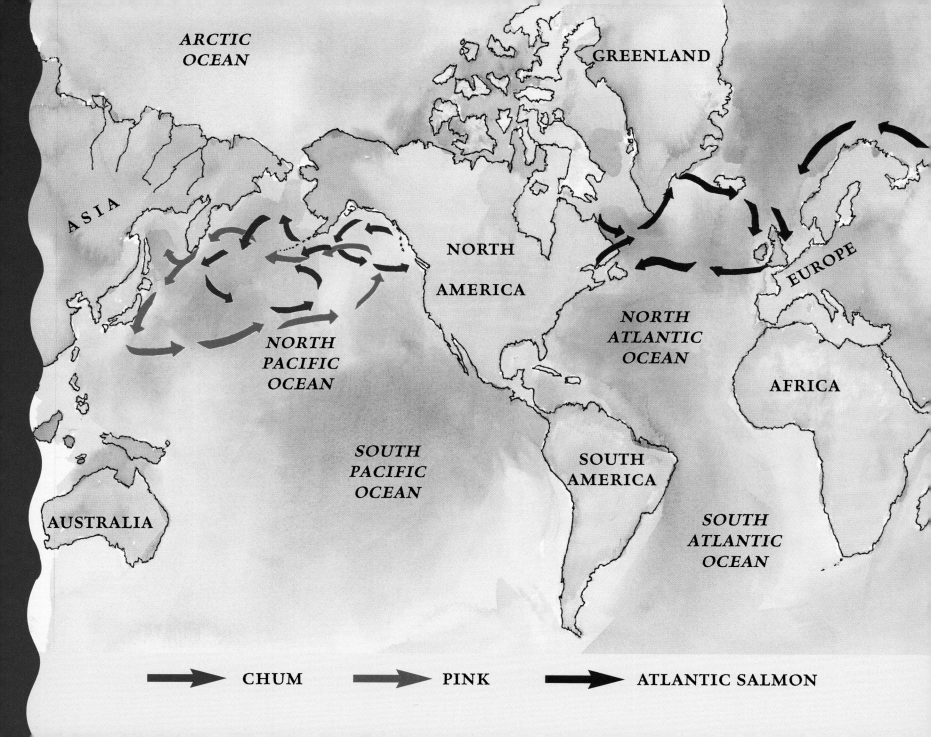

ARCTIC
OCEAN

GREENLAND

ASIA

NORTH
AMERICA

NORTH
PACIFIC
OCEAN

NORTH
ATLANTIC
OCEAN

EUROPE

AFRICA

SOUTH
PACIFIC
OCEAN

SOUTH
AMERICA

AUSTRALIA

SOUTH
ATLANTIC
OCEAN

CHUM   PINK   ATLANTIC SALMON

How Is the Pacific Salmon Run Different?

The life cycle of Pacific salmon is almost the same as its Atlantic Ocean kin. The great chinook usually travels long distances to spawn. The smaller chum and pink salmon spawn closer to the sea. Pacific salmon only spawn once. After they lay their eggs, both the males and females die. Only the steelhead may travel back to the ocean and survive to spawn again.

Who Eats Salmon?

Salmon are food for many animals. Bears, wolves, and eagles feast on them as the salmon travel through Canada and the United States. After they spawn and die, the salmon decay and supply nourishment for the stream. Fish, including trout, eat many of the eggs. The alevins and smolts also become food for larger fish. Out of three thousand eggs laid by a female, fewer than ten will survive to return to the home stream.

This Alaskan grizzly bear has caught a tasty meal.

People all over the world catch salmon because they are good to eat. Native Americans depended on salmon fishing to survive in the past and many still do today. More sockeye and pink are caught than any other type of salmon. Salmon are canned, smoked, and pickled. Their eggs are used for caviar. In Japan, salmon are used to make salmon paste, burgers, sausage, and soup.

The Chinook Indians chose the chinook salmon as a symbol to represent their people.

Where Have All the Salmon Gone?

Each year, fewer salmon are returning to their home streams. The Atlantic salmon no longer arrive in large numbers to swim up the Connecticut River. In Quebec and New Brunswick, the rivers are empty, too. There are no Atlantic salmon for the fishermen to catch. The Columbia River is no longer filled with squirming sockeye salmon. Few chinook swim into the Sacramento River in California.

NOTICE

THE MUNICIPALITY OF
ANCHORAGE RECOMMENDS
AGAINST THE EATING
OF FISH TAKEN FROM
THESE WATERS BECAUSE
OF CHEMICAL
CONTAMINATION OF
STREAM SEDIMENTS

DEPT. OF HEALTH AND HUMAN
SERVICES 264-4720

Many salmon cannot reach their home streams because dams block their path. Pollution from logging and mining may kill the fish, too. People cut down trees along the streams. Trees help the water to stay cool and also keep dirt from washing into the rivers. Without trees, water may become too warm or too muddy and the salmon cannot live. Because so many people prize salmon, they are fished in large numbers.

Dams, pollution, and overfishing are just some of the reasons that salmon have become extinct in many streams. If the salmon do not return, other animals that eat them, such as bears and eagles, may be hungry.

How Do Hatcheries and Fish Farms Help Salmon?

Some people think that fish hatcheries help salmon. Salmon eggs are raised in hatcheries until the fish become smolts. The hatcheries then release the smolts into the river to travel to the ocean. After three or four years, the salmon return to their home stream at the hatchery where they are captured and sold. Fish hatcheries in Japan and Russia release about 2.5 billion smolts into the Pacific Ocean each year.

Fish farms are a little different. On fish farms, salmon are raised from eggs to adults in pens along the coast. Salmon farming is so successful that sometimes farms grow more fish than people can catch.

How Do Hatcheries and Fish Farms Hurt Salmon?

Scientists are afraid that fish hatcheries may hurt the wild salmon. So many hatchery fish are being put in the ocean that they may eat all of the food in the ocean feeding grounds. Fish farms also cause problems. They pollute the water because the fish create a lot of waste. Salmon raised at hatcheries and farms are weaker than the salmon that grow up in rivers and oceans. No one is sure what will happen if the two types mix together. There is still a lot that we do not understand about salmon and how they live in the ocean.

These hatchery-raised smolts are just the right size
to be released into the river.

What Can You Do to Help Salmon?

Many people care about salmon. They are trying to help the salmon reach their home streams. Dams are being built with fish ladders to help the salmon travel upstream. In Idaho and Washington, migrating smolts hitch a ride from the Snake River down to the Columbia River. Wildlife biologists carry them in barges, past the dams, so that they are closer to the ocean. Sometimes, the best thing to do is to get rid of a dam. Edward's Dam was built on the Kennebec River in Augusta, Maine, in 1837. On July 1, 1999, Edward's Dam was removed so that Atlantic salmon could once again reach their spawning grounds.

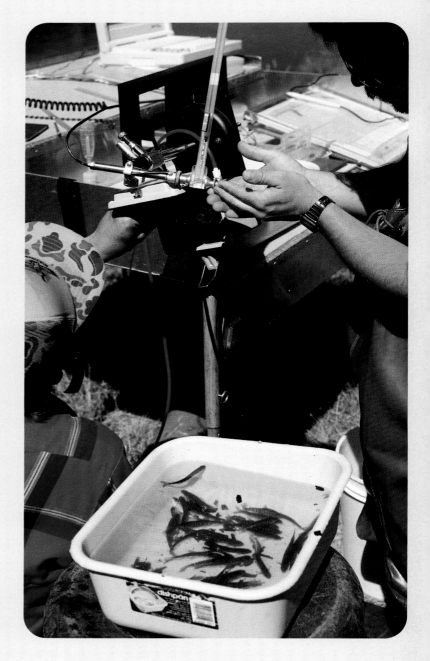

Scientists study salmon fry to learn more about migration.

You can help salmon by working to clean up streams. You can also plant trees on the riverbanks to keep the water shady and cool. New laws are being made to protect the salmon. The laws tell fishermen how many salmon they can take from the ocean and rivers. We must continue to do all of these things to help save the salmon.

Glossary

alevin - baby salmon that are less than 1 inch long (2.50 cm); alevins live in the gravel and feed off of their yolk sac

extinct - something that no longer exists

fish ladder - a ladder in which the steps are pools of water that allow a fish to swim past a dam, by going over it or around it

fry - baby salmon up to 4 inches (10 cm) long that feed on insects

migration - movement from one place to another; a salmon migration may be from the ocean feeding grounds to the home stream

parr - young salmon that are 4–5 inches (10–13 cm) long and brownish in color; parr remain in freshwater streams and have parr marks, which are black stripes on the sides of their bodies that help with camouflage

redd - a large nest made by the female salmon

run - a fish migration

smolt - juvenile salmon, 4–8 inches (10–20 cm) long, that leave the river and swim to the ocean; all smolts have parr marks except for pink salmon

spawn - releasing eggs and sperm